Insights of
Jesus

Written and compiled by
Andrea Skevington

A Lion Book
an imprint of
Lion Hudson plc
Mayfield House, 256 Banbury Road,
Oxford OX2 7DH, England
www.lionhudson.com
ISBN-13: 978-0-7459-5216-1
ISBN-10: 0-7459-5216-X

First edition 2006
10 9 8 7 6 5 4 3 2 1 0

Picture acknowledgments

pp. 6–7, 20, 22–23, 30–31, 36–37,
40–41, 43, 46–7, 48 copyright ©
Digital Vision; pp. 8, 10, 12–13, 16–17,
27, 28–29, 34 copyright © Alamy Ltd;
p. 33 copyright © Jonathan Self.

Text acknowledgments

pp. 9, 10, 11, 14, 15, 17, 18, 21, 24,
25, 27, 32, 35, 36, 39, 40 and 44 are
Scripture quotations taken from the Holy
Bible, New International Version,
copyright © 1973, 1978, 1984
International Bible Society. Used by
permission of Zondervan and Hodder
and Stoughton Limited. All rights
reserved.

pp. 19 and 23 are Scripture quotations
taken from the Holy Bible, English
Standard Version, published by Harper
Collins Publishers, copyright © 2001
Crossway Bibles, a division of Good
News Publishers. Used by permission.
All rights reserved.

pp. 22 and 26 are Scripture quotations
taken from the Holy Bible, New Living
Translation, copyright © 1996. Used by
permission of Tyndale House Publishers,
Inc., Wheaton, Illinois 60189. All rights
reserved.

pp. 30, 31, 38, 41, 45 and 47 are
Scripture quotations taken from The
New American Standard Bible, copyright
© 1960, 1962, 1963, 1968, 1971,
1972, 1973, 1975, 1977, 1995 by The
Lockman Foundation. Used by
permission.

p. 35 is a Scripture quotation taken from
the Holman Christian Standard Bible
[HCSB]. Used by permission. All rights
reserved.

pp. 37, 42, 45 and 48 are Scripture
quotations taken from the
Contemporary English Version, copyright
© 1995 by American Bible Society.
Used by permission.

A catalogue record for this book is
available from the British Library

Typeset in Helvetica Neue Light

Printed and bound in China

Contents

Introduction

For as long as human beings have had the capacity to think and to dream, they have asked questions and searched for meaning in their lives. Many have tried to answer these questions and to find God.

When Jesus began his work, he spoke in a time when people were trying to work their way to God up a slippery ladder of rules. They were amazed when they heard Jesus speak, because his teaching was so different to all that they had heard before. It addresses the big questions and looks at the motives from which actions spring – the sources of love, hope and fulfilment. His words provide some surprising answers.

For although Jesus' teaching is full of profound and practical advice for how to live a good and fulfilling life, there is far more to it than that. Jesus did not just seek to give answers to people's questions – he claimed to be the answer. He claimed to be the Way, and the Truth and the Life itself.

How he lived and died, as well as what he said, opened the door to heaven, and allowed us to see the light streaming through into our ordinary lives. Ordinary lives that are prized by God, and precious to him beyond price.

In this book you will find just a few of these insights, the tiniest glimpse of something life-changing. May it give light to your days.

Love

Having loved his own who were in the world, he now showed them the full extent of his love.

John 13:1

Love and joy

Wherever Jesus went, in whatever he said and did, he demonstrated his great love. He lived an extraordinary life and died an extraordinary death, pouring out his love for all people. But he did more than that. He taught that the path of love was a revolutionary way of life open to us all – one that would be blessed by joy, and marked with suffering.

'As the Father has loved me, so have I loved you. Now remain in my love. If you obey my commands, you will

*remain in my love, just as I have obeyed my Father's
commands and remain in his love. I have told you this
so that my joy may be in you and that your joy may be
complete. My command is this: Love each other as I
have loved you. Greater love has no-one than this, that
he lay down his life for his friends.'*
John 15:9–13

Who is my neighbour?

We are often tempted to put limits on our love. We ask whom we should love, and how much. Jesus answered these questions by his life, as well as through his words.

> On one occasion an expert in the law stood up to test Jesus. 'Teacher,' he asked, 'what must I do to inherit eternal life?'
>
> 'What is written in the Law?' he replied. 'How do you read it?'
>
> He answered: ' "Love the Lord your God with all your heart and with all your soul and with all your strength and with all your mind"; and, "Love your neighbour as yourself." '
>
> 'You have answered correctly,' Jesus replied. 'Do this and you will live.'
>
> But he wanted to justify himself, so he asked Jesus, 'And who is my neighbour?'
>
> Luke 10:25–29

Love one another

Jesus knew that one of his closest friends was about to betray him. And yet we see him both loving and serving all the disciples in the most extraordinary way. He washed their feet – the job of the humblest slave. And then, he told them that it was by such love that they would be recognized as his followers.

When he had finished washing their feet, he put on his clothes and returned to his place. 'Do you understand what I have done for you?' he asked them. 'You call me "Teacher" and "Lord", and rightly so, for that is what I am. Now that I, your Lord and Teacher, have washed your feet, you also should wash one another's feet. I have set you an example that you should do as I have done for you...'

'A new commandment I give you: Love one another. As I have loved you, so you must love one another. By this all men will know that you are my disciples, if you love one another.'
John 13:12–15, 34–35

Love, worship and forgiveness

Jesus taught us to love each other. But he also taught that love was at the heart of our relationship with him. It is our natural response to all the love we have received.

Then he turned towards the woman and said to Simon, 'Do you see this woman? I came into your house. You did not give me any water for my feet, but she wet my feet with her tears and wiped them with her hair. You did not give me a kiss, but this woman, from the time I entered, has not stopped kissing my feet. You did not put oil on my head, but she has poured perfume on my feet. Therefore, I tell you, her many sins have been forgiven – for she loved much.'
Luke 7:44–47

Giving

From the fullness of his grace we have all received one blessing after another.

John 1:16

All are fed

Jesus showed us how to live generously. He shared his time, his wisdom and his healing power with all. In doing so, he transformed lives.

In the feeding of the five thousand, it would have been so easy for the boy to keep his picnic of loaves and fish for himself, but he did not. He handed them over to Jesus. Sometimes, we too can think we have little to offer. In this parable, we learn that even a little can accomplish much.

When Jesus looked up and saw a great crowd coming towards him, he said to Philip, 'Where shall we buy bread for these people to eat?' He asked this only to test him, for he already had in mind what he was going to do.

Philip answered him, 'Eight months' wages would not buy enough bread for each one to have a bite!'

Another of his disciples, Andrew, Simon Peter's brother, spoke up, 'Here is a boy with five small barley loaves and two small fish, but how far will they go among so many?'

Jesus said, 'Make the people sit down.' There was plenty of grass in that place, and the men sat down, about five thousand of them. Jesus then took the loaves, gave thanks, and distributed to those who were seated as much as they wanted. He did the same with the fish.

When they had all had enough to eat, he said to his disciples, 'Gather the pieces that are left over. Let nothing be wasted.' So they gathered them and filled twelve baskets with the pieces of the five barley loaves left over by those who had eaten.

John 6:5–13

You did it for me

We too are encouraged to live generously. Jesus told this parable to show how vital it is to live a generous life. For when we give, we give to Jesus.

'Then the King will say to those on his right, "Come, you who are blessed by my Father; take your inheritance, the kingdom prepared for you since the creation of the world. For I was hungry and you gave me something to eat, I was thirsty and you gave me something to drink, I was a stranger and you invited me in, I needed clothes and you clothed me, I was sick and you looked after me, I was in prison and you came to visit me."

'Then the righteous will answer him, "Lord, when did we see you hungry and feed you, or thirsty and give you something to drink? When did we see you a stranger and invite you in, or needing clothes and clothe you? When did we see you sick or in prison and go to visit you?"

'The King will reply, "I tell you the truth, whatever you did for one of the least of these brothers of mine, you did for me." '

Matthew 25:34–40

The widow's gift

The kind of giving Jesus valued was not for show, but was giving from a generous heart.

Jesus went over to the collection box in the Temple and sat and watched as the crowds dropped in their money. Many rich people put in large amounts. Then a poor widow came and dropped in two pennies. He called his disciples to him and said, 'I assure you, this poor widow has given more than all the others have given. For they gave a tiny part of their surplus, but she, poor as she is, has given everything she has.'
Mark 12:41–44

Give

The generous life is full of blessings. Giving to others opens our hearts up to receiving both from them and from God.

'Give, and it will be given to you. A good measure, pressed down, shaken together, running over, will be put into your lap. For with the measure you use it will be measured back to you.'
Luke 6:38

Forgiveness

'A bruised reed he will not break, and a smouldering wick he will not snuff out.'

Matthew 12:20

Who can forgive?

Forgiveness is at the heart of Jesus' message. He came to bring God's forgiveness to us, thus setting us free. When Jesus healed the paralyzed man, he showed his authority to forgive us.

Seeing their faith, Jesus said to the paralyzed man, 'My son, your sins are forgiven.'

But some of the teachers of religious law who were sitting there said to themselves, 'What? This is blasphemy! Who but God can forgive sins!'

Jesus knew what they were discussing among themselves, so he said to them, 'Why do you think this is blasphemy? Is it easier to say to the paralyzed man, "Your sins are forgiven" or "Get up, pick up your mat, and walk"? I will prove that I, the Son of Man, have the authority on earth to forgive sins.' Then Jesus turned to the paralyzed man and said, 'Stand up, take your mat, and go on home, because you are healed!'

Mark 2:5–11

Restoring what is lost

In the story of the prodigal son, we see an example of the father's generosity and willingness to forgive those who come back to him. He reached out to both of his sons, wanting them to be included in the celebrations. The older brother's bitterness and his lack of forgiveness left him out in the cold, unable to join in the feast.

The younger son, the one who is sorry, returned home:

But while he was still a long way off, his father saw him and felt compassion, and ran and embraced him and kissed him. And the son said to him, 'Father, I have sinned against heaven and before you. I am no longer worthy to be called your son.' But the father said to his servants, 'Bring quickly the best robe, and put it on him, and put a ring on his hand, and shoes on his feet. And bring the fattened calf and kill it, and let us eat and celebrate. For this my son was dead, and is alive again; he was lost, and is found.' And they began to celebrate.

Now his older son was in the field, and as he came and drew near to the house, he heard music and dancing. And he called one of the servants and asked what these things meant. And he said to him, 'Your brother has come, and your father has killed the fattened calf, because he has received him back safe and sound.' But he was angry and refused to go in. His father came out and entreated him, but he answered his father, 'Look, these many years I have served you, and I never disobeyed your command, yet you never gave me a young goat, that I might celebrate with my friends. But when this son of yours came, who has devoured your property with prostitutes, you killed the fattened calf for him!' And he said to him, 'Son, you are always with me, and all that is mine is yours. It was fitting to celebrate and be glad, for this your brother was dead, and is alive; he was lost, and is found.'

Luke 15:20–32

Teach us to pray

When Jesus taught his followers to pray, he made sure that forgiveness was at the heart of the prayer. And he reminded them that God's forgiveness cannot help us if our own hearts are hard and cold towards those who have hurt us.

'This is how you should pray:
"Our Father in heaven,
hallowed be your name,
your kingdom come,
your will be done
on earth as it is in heaven.
Give us today our daily bread.
Forgive us our debts,
as we also have forgiven our debtors.
And lead us not into temptation,
but deliver us from the evil one."
For if you forgive men when they sin against you,
your heavenly Father will also forgive you.'
Matthew 6:9–14

From the Heart

'The good man brings good things out of the good stored up in his heart, and the evil man brings evil things out of the evil stored up in his heart. For out of the overflow of his heart his mouth speaks.'

Luke 6:45

Look to your heart

Jesus' teaching astonished those who heard it. The religious teaching of the time was full of detailed rules about right behaviour – and many of those rules emphasized what *not* to do. Jesus looked inside people, to understand their motives. He taught us to examine ourselves, and to think and to do right.

'You have heard that the law of Moses says, "Do not murder. If you commit murder, you are subject to judgment." But I say, if you are angry with someone, you are subject to judgment!'
Matthew 5:21–22

Beginning again?

When Nicodemus, a teacher and an expert in the ways of God, went to see Jesus, he challenged him with some extraordinary teaching. In response, Jesus showed that we must allow God to remake us, so that our hearts will be full of good things. Those who are born in this way will be moved by the Spirit, the way a boat is moved by the wind.

Now there was a man of the Pharisees named Nicodemus, a member of the Jewish ruling council. He came to Jesus at night and said, 'Rabbi, we know you are a teacher who has come from God. For no one could perform the miraculous signs you are doing if God were not with him.'

In reply Jesus declared, 'I tell you the truth, unless a man is born again, he cannot see the kingdom of God.'

'How can a man be born when he is old?'
Nicodemus asked. 'Surely he cannot enter a second
time into his mother's womb to be born!'
    Jesus answered, 'I tell you the truth, unless a man
is born of water and the Spirit, he cannot enter the
kingdom of God. Flesh gives birth to flesh, but the
Spirit gives birth to spirit. You should not be surprised
at my saying, "You must be born again." The wind
blows wherever it pleases. You hear its sound, but
you cannot tell where it comes from or where it is
going. So it is with everyone born of the Spirit.'
John 3:1–8

The good Samaritan

In the parable of the good Samaritan, we have an insight into the motive of the Samaritan: 'he felt compassion' for the wounded man, and it was this compassion that moved him to act as he did. Jesus placed value on compassion, and the mercy which flows from it.

'A man was going down from Jerusalem to Jericho, and fell among robbers, and they stripped him and beat him,

and went away leaving him half dead. And by chance a priest was going down on that road, and when he saw him, he passed by on the other side. Likewise a Levite also, when he came to the place and saw him, passed by on the other side.

'But a Samaritan, who was on a journey, came upon him; and when he saw him, he felt compassion, and came to him and bandaged up his wounds, pouring oil and wine on them; and he put him on his own beast, and brought him to an inn and took care of him.

'On the next day he took out two denarii and gave them to the innkeeper and said, "Take care of him; and whatever more you spend, when I return I will repay you."

'Which of these three do you think proved to be a neighbour to the man who fell into the robbers' hands?'

And he said, 'The one who showed mercy towards him.' Then Jesus said to him, 'Go and do the same.'
Luke 10:30–37

Treasure Beyond Price

*'I came that they may have life,
and have it abundantly.'*

John 10:10

The treasure and the pearl

Jesus told these two jewel-like stories, which show our
desire for something beyond the everyday. They show us
that, in God, we can find treasure beyond our imaginings.

'The kingdom of heaven is like treasure hidden in a field. When a man found it, he hid it again, and then in his joy went and sold all he had and bought that field.

'Again, the kingdom of heaven is like a merchant looking for fine pearls. When he found one of great value, he went away and sold everything he had and bought it.'
Matthew 13:44–46

Welcomed into God's family

When Zacchaeus climbed a tree just to get a glimpse of Jesus, he too was looking for something. He found astonishing riches, greater than anything he had hoped for.

There was a man named Zacchaeus who was a chief tax collector, and he was rich. He was trying to see who Jesus was, but he was not able because of the crowd, since he was a short man. So running ahead, he climbed up a sycamore tree to see Jesus, since he was about to pass that way. When Jesus came to the place, he looked up and said to him, 'Zacchaeus, hurry and come down, because today I must stay at your house.'

So he quickly came down and welcomed him

joyfully. All who saw it began to complain, 'He's gone to lodge with a sinful man!'

But Zacchaeus stood there and said to the Lord, 'Look, I'll give half of my possessions to the poor, Lord! And if I have extorted anything from anyone, I'll pay back four times as much!'

'Today salvation has come to this house,' Jesus told him, 'because he too is a son of Abraham. For the Son of Man has come to seek and to save the lost.'
Luke 19:2–10

God first

Jesus taught us the way of trust.

'Therefore I tell you, do not worry about your life, what you will eat or drink; or about your body, what you will wear. Is not life more important than food, and the body more important than clothes? Look at the birds of the air; they do not sow or reap or store away in barns, and yet your heavenly Father feeds them. Are you not much more valuable than they?

'But seek first his kingdom and his righteousness, and all these things will be given to you as well.'
Matthew 6:25–26, 33

Treasure in heaven

The treasures of the kingdom are real and lasting. Our time and energy is so easily taken up by things that do not last, and that ultimately do not satisfy.

> *'Do not store up for yourselves treasures on earth, where moth and rust destroy, and where thieves break in and steal. But store up for yourselves treasures in heaven, where moth and rust do not destroy, and where thieves do not break in and steal. For where your treasure is, there your heart will be also.'*
> *Matthew 6:19–21*

The gift of peace

Jesus tried to prepare his followers for their lives after his death, and John's Gospel gives a superbly full account of his teaching at this time. He talks of the great gift of peace, and the coming of the Holy Spirit.

'I have told you these things while I am still with you. But the Holy Spirit will come and help you, because the Father will send the Spirit to take my place. The Spirit will teach you everything and will remind you of what I said while I was with you. I give you peace, the kind of peace that only I can give. It isn't like the peace that this world can give. So don't be worried or afraid.'
John 14:25–27

A Man of Sorrows

Seeing the people, he felt compassion for them, because they were distressed and dispirited like sheep without a shepherd.

Matthew 9:36

Blessings

Jesus had a compassionate heart, which knew grief and trouble. He reached out to those who were 'distressed and dispirited', giving them hope and showing them the way to greener, happier pastures.

Now when he saw the crowds, he went up on a mountainside and sat down. His disciples came to him, and he began to teach them, saying:

'Blessed are the poor in spirit,
for theirs is the kingdom of heaven.
Blessed are those who mourn,
for they will be comforted.
Blessed are the meek,
for they will inherit the earth.
Blessed are those who
hunger and thirst for righteousness,
for they will be filled.
Blessed are the merciful,
for they will be shown mercy.'
Matthew 5:1–7

His heart went out to her

Jesus' healing was motivated by his compassion. When he saw the heavy loss of the widow of Nain – the death of her only son – he was filled with sorrow for her. The people who saw Jesus raising the young man from the dead were right in what they said: 'God has come to help his people.'

Soon afterwards, Jesus went to a town called Nain, and his disciples and a large crowd went along with him. As he approached the town gate, a dead person was being carried out – the only son of his mother, and she was a widow. And a large crowd from the town was with her. When the Lord saw her, his heart went out to her and he said, 'Don't cry.'

Then he went up and touched the coffin, and those carrying it stood still. He said, 'Young man, I say to you, get up!' The dead man sat up and began to talk, and Jesus gave him back to his mother.

They were all filled with awe and praised God. 'A great prophet has appeared among us,' they said. 'God has come to help his people.'

Luke 7:11–16

Keep watch for me

As Jesus prepared for his arrest and death, we see him bearing a heavy load of grief. He does not walk away from the sorrow and pain before him: he asks God for the strength to endure. He tells his followers to do the same, but they cannot keep awake. Despite their weakness, he does not condemn them.

And he said to them, 'My soul is deeply grieved to the point of death; remain here and keep watch.'

And he went a little beyond them, and fell to the ground and began to pray that if it were possible, the hour might pass him by.

And he was saying, 'Abba! Father! All things are possible for you; remove this cup from me; yet not what I will, but what you will.'

And he came and found them sleeping, and said to Peter, 'Simon, are you asleep? Could you not keep watch for one hour?

'Keep watching and praying that you may not come into temptation; the spirit is willing, but the flesh is weak.'

Again he went away and prayed, saying the same words.

And again he came and found them sleeping, for their eyes were very heavy; and they did not know what to answer him.

Mark 14:34–40

Calm

There are times when we are afraid; when trouble and sorrow are poised to overwhelm us. It is then that we need to call out for help, and we will be heard.

Suddenly a windstorm struck the lake. Waves started splashing into the boat, and it was about to sink.

Jesus was in the back of the boat with his head on a pillow, and he was asleep. His disciples woke him and said, 'Teacher, don't you care that we're about to drown?'

Jesus got up and ordered the wind and the waves to be quiet. The wind stopped, and everything was calm.

Jesus asked his disciples, 'Why were you afraid? Don't you have any faith?'

Now they were more afraid than ever and said to each other, 'Who is this? Even the wind and the waves obey him!'

Mark 4:37–41

Come, Follow Me

'I am the way and the truth and the life. No one comes to the Father except through me.'

John 14:6

Following

Jesus' mission was not just to point the way to God, but to *be* the way to God. His teaching was full of deep insights, and his miracles transformed lives, but he was offering more than that. He was offering himself, and asking his followers to take part in this new way of living.

Going on from there he saw two other brothers, James the son of Zebedee, and John his brother, in the boat with Zebedee their father, mending their nets; and he called them.

Immediately they left the boat and their father, and followed him.

Jesus was going throughout all Galilee, teaching in their synagogues and proclaiming the gospel of the kingdom, and healing every kind of disease and every kind of sickness among the people.

Matthew 4:21–23

Easy to bear

Jesus the carpenter would have made yokes for the ox or ass who pulled the plough. He would have made the yoke to fit the shape and temperament of each animal. He knows his followers too, giving them an easy load to bear.

'If you are tired from carrying heavy burdens, come to me and I will give you rest. Take the yoke I give you. Put it on your shoulders and learn from me. I am gentle and humble, and you will find rest. This yoke is easy to bear, and this burden is light.'

Matthew 11:28–30

Good building

Jesus taught that it was important to *do* what was right, not just to hear and understand. He had been teaching his followers many things, and when he finished his teaching, he told a story to encourage them to take action as a result of his teachings.

'Everyone who comes to me and hears my words and acts on them, I will show you whom he is like:

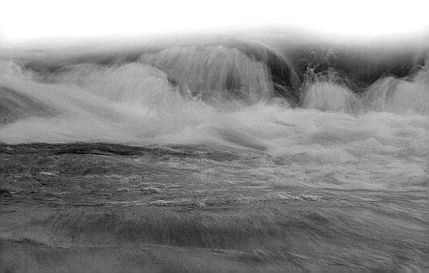

He is like a man building a house, who dug deep and laid a foundation on the rock; and when a flood occurred, the torrent burst against that house and could not shake it, because it had been well built.

'But the one who has heard and has not acted accordingly, is like a man who built a house on the ground without any foundation; and the torrent burst against it and immediately it collapsed, and the ruin of that house was great.'

Luke 6:47–49

I am the light

Jesus' followers were often full of questions. Jesus' priority was to show the way by what he did. He said he was the light by which the work of God could be done.

As Jesus walked along, he saw a man who had been blind since birth. Jesus' disciples asked, 'Teacher, why was this man born blind? Was it because he or his parents sinned?'

'No, it wasn't!' Jesus answered. 'But because of his blindness, you will see God work a miracle for him. As long as it is day, we must do what the one who sent me wants me to do. When night comes, no one can work. While I am in the world, I am the light for the world.'

After Jesus said this, he spat on the ground. He made some mud and smeared it on the man's eyes. Then he said, 'Go and wash off the mud in Siloam Pool.' The man went and washed in Siloam, which means 'One Who Is Sent.' When he had washed off the mud, he could see.

John 9:1–7